N. HENNINGFELD

The Homeowner's Wildfire Safety Guidebook

Understanding Home Hardening, Defensible Space, and Insurance

First published by Adaptive Firescapes 2023

Copyright © 2023 by N. Henningfeld

All rights reserved. No part of this publication may be reproduced, stored or transmitted in any form or by any means, electronic, mechanical, photocopying, recording, scanning, or otherwise without written permission from the publisher. It is illegal to copy this book, post it to a website, or distribute it by any other means without permission.

Designations used by companies to distinguish their products are often claimed as trademarks. All brand names and product names used in this book and on its cover are trade names, service marks, trademarks and registered trademarks of their respective owners. The publishers and the book are not associated with any product or vendor mentioned in this book. None of the companies referenced within the book have endorsed the book.

Legal Disclaimer: All the information and checklists within these pages are intended to be a guide. There is no guarantee of home or individual survival during wildfire events. You understand that all natural disasters have an inherent level of risk, but that by utilizing this step by step guide, you can greatly improve your chances of survival for yourself, your family (and pets), and your home. Please visit our website for more information and reference guides.

Adaptive Firescapes is not responsible for any claims, losses, negotiations, or record keeping with your homeowners insurance or other legal entities. This guide has been designed to help - but cannot guarantee - the survival of any individual or property.

First edition

ISBN: 9798853560741

This book was professionally typeset on Reedsy. Find out more at reedsy.com

Contents

I   Welcome

1	Introduction to Wildfire	3
2	Home Hardening & The Immediate Zone (0-5 feet)	7
3	Intermediate Zone (5-30 feet)	24
4	The Extended Zone (30-100 feet)	32
5	Insurance	37

About the Author   41

I

Welcome

Welcome, and thank you for purchasing the Wildfire Home Safety Guide. Developing these materials has been a personal goal of mine since I witnessed the destruction in Paradise, CA in 2018. Since then, I've made it my personal mission to learn and practice everything in these pages so I can compile all of it in one easy place for homeowners and municipalities alike. In this first book, you'll have all the basic information you need to identify wildfire vulnerabilities on your property.

1

Introduction to Wildfire

Why are wildfires so bad now? Is it all because of climate change? What do we do about all of these problems? And what is the Home Ignition Zone Model of wildfire safety and why does it matter?

In a nutshell, the answer to the first question is .. simple. When the Americas were rediscovered in the 1400s, they were colonized by a number of empires and kingdoms that were neither familiar, nor accustomed, to fire at a landscape level.

When the Dutch, Spaniards, Swedes, and others started immigrating en masse, the fledgling governing bodies of the new colonies (and later the Federal Government of the United States of America) tried to suppress wildfire. This 'wild' fire that was practiced by Native tribes posed a threat to the wood buildings that made up their towns, and posed a financial threat to the forests now "owned" by logging and timber barons. Fire was only necessary when clearing land for agriculture or building. This new wave of inhabitants had no concept of fire for regeneration.

Fast forward to the late 1800s and early 1900s. Three major fires destroyed 3 towns:
  1. Peshtigo, WI (caused by railroad employees),
  2. Chicago, IL (someone knocking over a lantern in a hay barn),
  3. Wallace, ID (winds stirring up multiple fires thought to be caused by sparks from trains as well as lightning).

A young nation was thoroughly traumatized by wildfire in an era where cities and towns were mostly constructed from timber. This was in a time before lumber was treated for fire and weather resistance, and fire resistant building materials hadn't been developed yet. So the government decided that every wildfire was a risk and any Smoke Tower employee was to report any signs of ignition and have the fire out by 10am the following morning.

And thus began decades of wildfire suppression.

Over Billions of acres.

These billions of acres had adapted to regular intervals with fire. Ignition from lightning or Native Americans; the forests, prairies, and savannahs of the northern hemisphere didn't care. But when fire was eliminated, more species started to compete for the same amount of space. More generations of trees and shrubs started trying to grow on the same amount of land, use the same finite amount of water and canopy space to receive sunlight.

Forests became weak and diseased when individual trees couldn't get enough water, sunlight, or nutrients. Trees, grasses, and shrubs alike started to become overgrown; they would succumb to their parasitic fungi, insects, or other diseases.

Hundreds of millions of acres started to pile up dead and dying plant material. There were no regular fires to keep the forest floors clear, or the prairies safe from conifer encroachment.

And then Americans started moving into the suburbs. And the suburbs started expanding into these wild places that hadn't been actively managed in decades. These communities were disasters waiting to happen, and yet they ignored the warnings from the USFS and NFPA about the wildfire risks.

The 1960s and 1970s were a stark reminder of the ferocity of wildfire when it has decades of fuel build up. Then the 80s happened, and Americans experienced a decade of above average precipitation and forgot about the fiery nightmares.

Our short memory was about to be stoked again in the '90s. Fires returned. Reagan had slashed the USFS budget and almost destroyed the very heart of American Environmentalism. The USFS was by no means a perfect organization, but they were a fledgling department asked to do many opposing things, and were doing the best they could with what they had. Unfortunately, they did too little, too late… and wildfires started roaring back to life in the early 2000s, and became the Fire Industrial Complex by the 2010s.

The natural disaster we seem to be faced with may appear

insurmountable.

But the truth of the matter is: we can all do a little bit to protect ourselves and our communities. With a surprisingly small amount of work, we can transform a budding Era of Conflagration into something that resembles historic fire regimes and stays in our wildlands. We can protect ourselves and let mother nature reset the balance of our forests and grasslands. In combination with fuels reduction projects and reintegrating Indigenous Knowledge, we can save our landscapes before it's too late. We just have to be willing to put in a little bit of effort. If it saves our national treasures like Glacier NP, Zion, Wupatki National Monument, the Redwoods, and so many other places… would it be worth it? No one wants to vacation in a burned over matchstick forest. That wouldn't make for great photos or instagram content. So.

Let's go all in.

All it takes are a few small chores at home, helping our neighbors, and working with local forestry professionals to protect our home. 'Cause once it burns, there's nowhere else to go.

And it will burn. It's wildfire roulette for every community every summer. It's not if, but when. And the steps to prepare and survive the firestorm are listed here.

So let's begin.

2

Home Hardening & The Immediate Zone (0-5 feet)

People have always told me that the best way to eat an elephant is one bite at a time. While I don't think I'd like the taste of elephant, it does keep me in check when I get these wild ideas about how to save the world and thinking I have to do everything all at once. Because that's what I want to do. Life Mission: Save The World. At least, some part of it. And right now, the goal is: every resident of every landscape that could catch on fire. Because, why not, right? Someone's got to do it. It's been my dream since November 2018 when Paradise, CA burned over. I couldn't believe my eyes! In this day and age, we lost an *ENTIRE TOWN* to wildfire. Impossible! And people died!!

And not too long after, I learned that none of it needed to happen.

By the beauty of serendipity, I ended up in a class taught by renowned Fire Physicist Dr. Jack Cohen in Missoula, MT.

He was teaching us about his Home Ignition Zone Model of Wildfire Readiness. We call it HIZ for short. He has spent his life investigating the aftermath of urban conflagration (what it's called when entire neighborhoods or cities burn down) to determine the cause of structure loss. He spent decades studying wildfire and all its effects - fire behavior, fire weather, fire modeling, everything. From the time he was a young boy growing up in Arizona, he was obsessed with fire. And his obsession yielded answers that fell on deaf ears for decades. Now, after Paradise, Rodeo-Chediski, Boulder, and countless other wildfire disasters, people are starting to look for those answers.

To begin, we need to understand that wildfire disasters are, at their heart, structural ignition disasters. What do I mean by that? We assign different values to different kinds of wildfires. A 50,000 acre wildfire in the heart of a designated Wilderness is more likely to be forgotten by the end of a newscast than a 500 acre wildfire in Orange County. We value our homes and cars, the things necessary to our day to day life and function, more than we value some unseen forest. Which makes sense, from a psychological standpoint. But that reinforces the new definition of a wildfire disaster as one of structural ignitability. If we could have a wildfire pass by our neighborhood and not lose a single home, shed, or car, would we still call it a wildfire disaster?

I don't think we would.

So how do we prevent a home from burning down, and take a wildfire disaster and turn it into a wildfire event? What if urban conflagrations could become a thing of the past? What if annual wildfire disasters became part of our seasonal preparations like 'possibility of a blizzard and getting snowed in'? And we could anticipate and prepare for them, and still be safe?

That's the goal of HIZ work. Assessing the ignition potential of any given structure, and mitigating it.

For legal reasons, you won't hear someone say "eliminating it" or "fireproofing" something but we sure will stand by the science that says, with a few simple ignition reduction techniques, you can greatly reduce the chance your home will fall victim during an ember shower during a wildland-urban fire.

A lot of the material in this chapter is fairly technical. There are photos on the website, www.adaptivefirescapes.com, to help you picture different building materials and building styles. It's important you stick with me through this chapter because your roof and the sides of your home are your shields during wildfire: they're protecting you from burning gale force winds and an onslaught of embers that range in size from little specks to entire burning tree branches.

To start, let's review some definitions:
The Home Ignition Zone is the entire area one to two hundred feet out from the walls of your home, including the space above your roof.

Defensible Space is the buffer zone between a structure on your property and the tall grass, trees, shrubs, or wildland that surrounds it. This one-two hundred foot zone is critical for slowing down approaching fire to decrease its severity and intensity near your home. Ignition can occur from embers, direct flame contact, or radiant heat, which is when things get so hot, they combust, like aiming the light from the sun through a magnifying glass. This zone is not only critical for the survival of your home, but also for emergency vehicles to safely access your home to defend it. I'll discuss that more in chapter four.

Within the Home Ignition Zone, your property is broken down into three sub zones: the immediate zone, the intermediate zone, and the extended zone. The immediate zone needs to be as flame and ember resistant as possible. I won't say fireproof, because nothing is truly fireproof with a few stonework exceptions. If it gets hot enough, it will burn or melt, and I don't want to leave any room for misinterpretation or hungry lawyers.

The **immediate zone** is your house and any space 5 feet from the exterior walls. This includes any trees, vines, or tall shrubs touching or overhanging your roof and gutters, windowsills and decks. The immediate zone also includes any wood or composite decking or fencing that touches your home and could lead a grass fire right up the walls.

The **intermediate zone** encompasses the ground 5-30 feet away from your home. This is usually where you see nice manicured lawns and decorative landscaping.

The **extended zone** is anything beyond 30 feet. For urban areas we say 30-100 feet. For property owners in more rural areas, it's anything from 30 feet out to your property line, but at least one to two hundred feet.

The immediate zone is where we focus on all the Home

Hardening strategies, so let's start at the top and take stock of your roofing material.

Do you know what kind of shingles you have? Are they composite or ceramic? How old are they? Are there any shingles missing? Do you have wood shakes? Concrete or slate tiles? Metal panels? If you have metal panels, is your plywood sheathing thick enough that it won't combust underneath from the radiant heat? What is your underlayment rated to?

 These are all things you need to be thinking about when assessing your roof. If you don't know, have a roofing contractor come check it out for you. Or if you need to replace your roof, tell the contractor you need the new roof to be Class A or Class B rated, depending on your surroundings and your level of risk and exposure.

 What is Class A and Class B? Are there more classes? Yes. Building materials are rated as Class A, B, C, or unrated for fire resistance. Class A will be the most fire resistant, with C being the least fire resistant, and unrated should be avoided and won't even be discussed here.

Class A: Generally the preferred roofing for commercial buildings, and highly recommended in residential settings that are at high risk from wildfire. Class A is effective against severe fire exposure meaning it can withstand burning material up to one square foot weighing approximately four pounds, something approximately the size of a gallon of milk, and will resist ignition from radiant heat for 2-4 hours. It will allow for a maximum of 6 feet of flame spread once ignited. With Class A, you need to consider if the shingles or panels are stand alone rated, meaning you don't have to worry about your sheathing or underlayment, or if it's a Full Assembly Class A which means all components of your roof need to be carefully selected for it to achieve that Class A rating. Class A ceramic, stone, concrete, asphalt composite shingles are generally fine as stand alone. Consult with your contractor to make sure the correct grade is purchased as they can be offered in A, B, and C.

Metal panels need at least ½" plywood sheathing and other higher rated materials in order to reach a Class A Rating. Again, consult with your contractor to make sure all components are checked before the project begins. For commercial buildings, PVC and TPO are available in the Class A option, and some acrylic and silicone roofing coatings are available as a component of a Whole Roofing System to achieve that Class A Rating.

Class B Fire Rating is for moderate fire exposure. It can last 1 hour of exposure before ignition, withstand a burning brand that is 6 square inches and weighs up to one pound, so something like a paperback book or bag of coffee. In the event of ignition, it will experience a maximum of 8 feet of flame spread. Shakes and shingles are available in this option, and it is rarely used in commercial buildings.

Class C has minimal fire resistance. It can resist ignition for approximately 20 minutes, and withstand a one and a half square inch burning ember weighing a quarter of a gram. That doesn't mean much unless you're a scientist or a drug dealer, so let's put that into perspective: a standard paperclip is 1 gram and one and one eighths of an inch long. So an ember the size of your average tea bag (2 grams and about 2.5 inches long) could ignite your roof if you have a Class C rating. Examples of this include untreated wood shingles, untreated plywood and untreated particleboard.

Now that we've covered roofing materials, let's briefly discuss

HOME HARDENING & THE IMMEDIATE ZONE (0-5 FEET)

the style of your roof. Most common styles are gable, gambrel, pyramid, hip, and hip and valley. From here, depending on your preferred architectural style, you can add in dormers, dutch gables, additional peaks, change the slope of different portions and make your roof as complex and elaborate as you please. And this is where it gets fun. So at all those valleys, or the junctions of two different roof sections coming together, is where you get to talk to your roofer about if those valleys will be open or closed. Depending on the material you choose to cover your roof with, the manufacturer may make that choice for you, however, most shingles will offer you the choice of a closed valley, which is where both portions of roof come together and appear to blend seamlessly. The other option is an open valley with metal flashing. Not only does it provide better resistance to water penetration, but it helps shed debris faster than closed valleys. The choice between open and closed really comes down to cost and which style appeals to you more. However, it's being argued by some manufacturers that the open metal valleys make it faster and easier to clean your roof of combustible material like pine needles and other leaves due to lower static friction. But at the end of the day, it all comes down to cost and design preference.

Other roofing features to consider include chimneys, skylights, gutters, and vents. If you have a chimney or stovepipe outlet, make sure it has a spark arrestor screen with openings one sixteenth to three eighths of an inch. Consult with your local chimney technician to make sure that any screen you install allows for adequate exhaust if the fireplace or stove is being used. They can also answer any questions you have about chimney codes and regulations in your state.

Dual pane glass skylights with a screen offer the best protection compared to plastic dome skylights on a sloped roof. However, domed skylights offer the best protection from accumulated debris if placed on a flat roof. You also want to make sure skylights are installed with metal flashing for added protection from elements, debris build up and wildfire. And if you have a ventilating skylight (one that opens) make sure it has a screen and is closed tight in the event of an approaching wildfire.

Gutters. Everybody's favorite weekend chore. Keeping your gutters clear of debris is absolutely critical. Gutters are one of the biggest failure points on a home when it comes to raining embers. You have to have to have to HAVE TO keep your gutters cleaned or get enclosed gutters or gutter guards. Placing the recommended mesh over top is sufficient as long as you keep debris from building up and plugging the mesh. Also helpful is metal flashing around the edge of your roof. It's usually installed to act as an extra moisture barrier, but it turns out to be effective against small embers and small flames, too!

So can we use any kind of gutter, then? No. Plastic will melt and burn and the direct flame contact leads to ignition of roofing and siding material, so metal is going to be your best option. And whatever you do, DO NOT use the foam inserts for your gutters that claim to be fireproof. They are not. In informal testing by Fire Safe Marin, they are "highly combustible, ignite easily, and spread fire rapidly." It's important to keep your roof clear of debris as best you can before fire approaches. When winds pick up during the firestorm, new debris and burning material will be deposited on your roof. You want the best chance possible of your roof surviving the onslaught. If you have a Class A, some burning pine needles and small clumps of burning leaves won't get through your exterior. But there's no need to tempt fate with a roof covered in old debris.

Last but not least we have roofing vents. If you have exposed vents like ridge vents, off-ridge vents, box vents, turbines, or cupolas, make sure they have ember resistant screens across all openings, unless they were manufactured to resist wind driven rain and were built with an external baffle at the vent inlet. This is important for intake and exhaust vents as research conducted by the Insurance Institute for Business & Home Safety, or IBHS, showed that all vents become intake vents when the wind blows directly at them.

Now, there's a fine line to walk with screens on your vents. One eighth inch vents will allow sufficient air flow, but will also let in smaller embers that could ignite combustible material inside your home. However, if you get a smaller screen size, like one sixteenth inch mesh, it becomes quickly covered by debris and potentially halts all airflow in or out of your home unless cleaned regularly. It can also become plugged if it is accidentally painted over. So what do you do? Outside of replacing all your vents with new models that were specifically designed for wildfire, the one eighth inch is adequate as long as you keep unnecessary and fine combustible materials out of your attic or crawl space. That means no collection of crunchy magazines upstairs that you're keeping for nostalgic purposes.

Now some contractors may try to argue that these new wildfire vents don't allow for adequate airflow or weren't designed properly for older homes. Untrue. If airflow really is an issue, you can just add more vents or stick with the eighth inch mesh and keep your attic and crawl spaces clear of combustible material. In some states, homes built in 2008 or after, have already been built with wildfire resistant vents and have had their airflow calculated for these new vents. One thing to keep in mind when considering replacing any vents, is that off-ridge vents, gable end vents, crawl space vents, and open eave vents have the highest potential to see flame because of the increased chance of combustible material getting deposited in and around these spaces. Be sure to keep them clear and surrounded by fire resistant siding when possible.

Siding options for your home come in 2 classes: combustible and non-combustible. And remember too, like in roofing, there are ignition resistant materials, and ignition resistant construction.

Starting off with non combustible materials: we've got metal, stone, three coat stucco, and fiber cement. Combustible siding is everything else: solid wood and wood composite (osb or plywood), vinyl, and vinyl composite. That list comprises most people's homes, but that doesn't mean you're up a creek without a paddle if your home isn't made of stone or metal. You can have combustible siding, but if it was constructed in such a way as to be ignition resistant, AND you follow the rules for firescaping your 0-5 and 5-30 foot zones, you can still be considered *ignition resistant*.

If you have vinyl or composite siding, make sure they're tongue-and-groove design, rather than a simple bevel overlay. When the pieces fit together, any possible firebrands or embers that find their way between the boards are more likely to burn out before they burn through and ignite the interior sheathing which, like your roofing sheathing, is hopefully a half inch thick to provide the best structure and ignition resistance.

Or, you can look into other sheathing options like gypsum board commonly known as drywall, particularly if you have the budget to get X-Type Fire Resistant boards. But again, don't fret too much about your siding, because the flame front near your home only lasts about 5-10 minutes during an urban wildfire, and most siding can withstand those temps for about 20 minutes.

If you have a home in a rural area you're surrounded by trees on all sides, you'll need to ensure your canopy spacing meets requirements all the way out to 100 feet or more. Generally, your biggest concerns will still be vegetation and other combustible materials allowing for direct flame contact or prolonged exposure to open flame.

With proper firescaping, most siding will survive a wildfire, at least to the degree that your home will still be there when you get back. It is not unreasonable to plan to have your melted vinyl siding replaced when you return. However, if you have other structures close to your house that are made of combustible materials, including neighbors or detached garages, you may want to consider non combustible siding.

Just to touch on it briefly: at this time, gels, intumescent paints, stains, and other coatings are not effective in long term safety or for prolonged exposure to heat or flame. Some gels are being developed but their long term efficacy is unknown and should not be counted on to save your home, with or without proper vegetation management.

Windows. Old houses have single pane windows. I remember a big push when I was growing up for people to upgrade to energy efficient, better insulated, dual pane tempered glass windows. Besides helping insulate your home better year round, it turns out these new windows are also FOUR TIMES more resistant to breaking during wildfire than single pane windows. Combine that with one sixteenth inch window screens, and you'll be ready.

If you want to take it one step further, especially if you have single pane windows and can't afford to upgrade, consider adding shutters, or mounting hardware around your windows so you can place half in thick plywood over them for an added layer of protection. Make sure all vegetation and possible ladder fuels that could ignite the plywood or shutters is removed. Some organizations recommend moving all furniture and window curtains to the center of the room, away from windows, but radiant heat coming through a double pane window experiences a 50-75% drop in temperature and heat transfer.

Now windows can get surprisingly complicated so I'll try to keep it simple. As you may know, you have many options for framing materials, glass type, and glass coatings. If you've ever been to a home improvement store and designed your own windows, it might've felt overwhelming. You can choose between wood, aluminum, vinyl, or mixed material frames, which all have their own risks and benefits in wildfire exposure studies.

Studies have shown that some vinyls are susceptible to warping during high radiant heat exposure and can allow for the glass pane to fall out of the frame long before the glass ever cracks. However, there are vinyl windows that are designed with additional structural support and comply with various national window standards and specifications, so you can more safely rely on them during a wildfire.

Look for specifications such as the American Architectural Manufacturers Association AAMA 101, Window & Door Manufacturers Association WDMA I.S.2, or Canadian Standards Association CSA A440-08. You can get single, double, or triple pane windows, which of course, standard recommendations advise double pane protection or better. Tempered glass is the best, annealed and laminated glass are the least effective in surviving heat stress and will fail at lower radiant heat temperatures.

Glass coatings and reflective films have been shown to improve glass performance. Just make sure you have a 1/16th inch mesh window screen installed in the event of breakage so you have an added layer of protection. In addition, there have been reports around the country, featured on news stations in New York, North Carolina, and California, that Low E glass windows have melted lawn furniture, ignited mulch, and burned plants and humans alike. So, if you have new windows installed and you notice your neighbors siding starting to melt, please be proactive and work with your neighbor to repair it and prevent further damage. Call the window company and have it replaced with something less dangerous. We are supposed to be in the business of preventing fire and helping each other, not accidentally lighting each other's homes on fire because we have a defective or dangerous window.

Now with regards to reflective films, research out of Australia in 2006 showed some increased benefit, but all of my subsequent searches of reflective window tint didn't yield any information, so check with your local window installers and centers for energy efficiency on the latest advancements.

Decks, patios, covered porches, and gazebos. All of these things must be clear of combustible vegetation. If you have decorative vines growing up and around your deck or arbor, that is a ladder fuel, and will bring fire right up to your home. You can have a wooden deck or gazebo, but do consider upgrading to composite, or a non combustible material if your budget allows, when the time comes for it to be replaced. Make sure you keep the deck boards clear of leaves and other outdoor dust bunnies. Always check the corners and crevices for piles of combustible material.

One thing that can help greatly during high winds and raining embers, is to have metal flashing between your deck and your home. It's a typical piece of construction that adds an extra layer of protection from the elements and turns out to be great for wildfire resistance. In a similar vein, having concrete foot pads for your deck posts gives you an added bit of protection from surrounding vegetation or any firebrands that may collect around your deck posts. Depending on how high off the ground your deck is, you'll want to add one eighth inch mesh underneath it, or behind your decorative lattice to keep embers from getting under it and igniting the deck from below. You'll want to make sure that all vegetation is cleared out from underneath and any animal nests are removed. Whether your deck or porch is a foot off the ground, or 6 feet off the ground, it is absolutely critical to remove all combustible material, particularly those that could carry a tall flame.

One more thing to consider with decks, porches, or patios, is what kind of furniture you have on it. Grills, small propane tanks, stacks of firewood, wicker furniture, and so on. If fire is inbound, you want to get everything off your deck or porch. Firewood should ALWAYS be at least 30 feet from the home during wildfire season, and given a ten foot space around and above it in case it ignites. Best practice is to not stack it beside or in between trees, so that if it does ignite, it doesn't burn those trees down with it.

Career firefighters have reported that many homes ignite because of the firewood stacked beside or simply too close to the house. There are fire resistant tarps available on the market, but keep in mind, they're fire resistant, not fireproof, and they do not make a good substitute for moving stacks of firewood at least 30 feet away from the home. During rain or snow, it's fine to have some wood closer, but keep in mind how hot it burns with 3 or 4 pieces in your stove - you don't want an entire pile of it burning right next to your home. All that radiant heat will further stress the materials on the exterior of the house.

That goes for trash and recycling too. Get those cans and tubs away from the house if fire is approaching. Anything else that might be alongside the house between the fence and the back wall: kids toys, kayaks, old wood projects, random junk that got shoved in back and willfully forgotten about. Move it inside the house, shed, or garage, or get it 30 feet away. That goes for cars, boats, motorcycles, and RVs too. There have been times where someone's vehicle has ignited on the concrete driveway, but the house survived because there was adequate distance between the two. Think how hot a vehicle would burn. You don't want that right next to the house.

Congratulations! You've made it to the home stretch.

Fences and gates. Again: anything that touches the home, is the home. You don't have to rush out and replace your entire fence if it's made of wood, vinyl, or composite. But the gate or portion of the fence that touches the house….needs to be fire resistant. You don't want a grass fire igniting your wooden privacy fence, just to watch the flame travel along and go right up to the side of your house. You want to keep flames a minimum of 5 feet away, and keep anything with an extended burn time at least 30 feet away. But in the case of something like a fence, if possible, you want it even farther still. Sustained burning of combustible material too close to the house will increase the chance of home ignition. Consider a 6 foot privacy fence that you convert to chain link or aluminum posts within the immediate, and part way into the intermediate zone. If the 6 foot boards are burning and they fall over, they could fall directly into your siding. Direct flame contact on anything other than metal or stone will cause ignition.

So keep fences as non combustible as possible. I know metal prices and building material costs are only going up and it's much easier to say that than actually afford to do it. But maybe this is our chance to work with our insurance companies and have them help with home hardening upgrades or work something out on our policy costs or coverage now that we have this data driven scientific model to show that small changes make a big difference. Another option for financial assistance is to work with your local Office of Emergency Management, USFS, DNRC, FireWise, or similar organizations. There is grant money available to help, and these agencies are trying to find homeowners in need of them.

This is our chance to write our future. Let's be smart and start with these changes while we have this window of opportunity. If we all take the initiative and work together, we can not just survive wildfire, but thrive afterwards.

For up to date recommendations on wildfire systems, visit us on social media or our website. We regularly check for new retrofit options and often have competitive prices on the best products through our online store (coming soon).

3

Intermediate Zone (5-30 feet)

Now we get to talk about my favorite part: firescaping! It's here in your intermediate and extended zones that you get to let your artistic vision have a heyday. Now I know a lot of you probably have these wonderful junglescapes in your backyard that give you happy cottage vibes when you come home. And I can appreciate wanting to peer out the window through a bunch of leaves and branches and feel like you're in your own private oasis. Unfortunately, in today's world, that's becoming a huge liability. That's not to say you can't have your oasis, but it means you have to weigh the pros and cons and be honest with yourself on your level of risk tolerance. Your insurance company will have something to say about it too....

First I want to make it crystal clear that firescaping DOES NOT mean that you have to get rid of all your flowers, trees, and shrubs. It does not mean you have to bury your lawn or garden in pea gravel or pave it over with flagstones. As we discussed in the last chapter, you just have to keep the plants away from the sides of your home.

INTERMEDIATE ZONE (5-30 FEET)

Keep your beautiful landscaping. Keep your manicured property. But follow a few simple rules to ensure it's the most fire tolerant and resilient landscape it can be. So let's start with some definitions and ground rules.

Defensible Space: this is the buffer zone between the house and the wildlands around it. It's the area firefighters need to have clear and properly managed in order to stand between the flame front and your home. Ideally it would be 100 feet, but sometimes in more urban areas it's as little as 30-50 feet. This also includes your driveway and road access, a locked driveway gate, any sharp turns or steep grades on your driveway. We'll get into more detail on that later in this episode.

Plant spacing: the recommended vertical and horizontal distance between plants to keep a crown fire from spreading.

Ladder Fuels: as you may have inferred from the name, ladder fuels are any combustible materials that will carry flame from the ground, up into another source that would otherwise have been safe from ground level flames. Examples include shrubs or young trees growing directly beneath mature trees, or vines or bushes growing in or around your deck or siding.

Fuel Types: We have One hour, Ten hour, Hundred hour, and Thousand hour fuels. These are particularly important because they play a major role in predicting how your property, or different parts of it, will burn. The time frame in the name denotes how quickly the fuel type will dry out in an open environment.

One Hour Fuels are anything a quarter inch in diameter or smaller. That's not the length of it, but how thick it is. For example, mulch, grasses, leaf litter, those are all one hour fuels. Small combustibles will dry out faster and be the most susceptible to embers and radiant heat. Now, I am not anti-mulch, so we'll discuss different kinds of mulch and how they burn so you can make your own informed decision on what you want to landscape with.

Ten Hour Fuels are an inch or smaller in diameter. This still includes mulch, grasses, leaf litter, and starts to factor in smaller twigs and branches. This means that in warm, windy conditions, these materials will get crispy in ten hours or less. Prime fuel for a fire. Think about all the little pieces of leaf, grass, or woody material you collect when you're out camping and you're trying to start a fire with the tiniest of sparks. Those are your one and ten hour fuels. With that in mind, you can see why you don't want those right next to your home, or in large, continuous swaths around your property.

Hundred Hour Fuels are 1-3 inches in diameter. Examples include saplings and medium sized branches.

Thousand Hour Fuels are anything between 3-8 inches in diameter. That would include young trees and large branches from more mature trees. Don't be fooled by the name, though. Just because 100 and 1000 hour fuels take longer to dry out, doesn't mean they're less dangerous. You'll often find these fuel types piled up in forests from previous natural disasters such as windstorms, avalanches and landslides, and previous fires. Other times you may see fuel types like these are in burn piles

INTERMEDIATE ZONE (5-30 FEET)

on properties that are actively mitigating their fuel loads. If this is something you're interested in starting on your property, I'll give you some basics to help you get started.

Firescaping: designing a landscape such that it will decrease the severity and intensity of an approaching fire.

Xeriscaping: utilizing native plants, or nonnatives that are adapted to a similar environment (similar water regimes, fire regimes, and annual sun and precipitation patterns) to create a landscape that is completely or mostly self-sustaining without the need for additional irrigation.

Now that we've got that out of the way, let's talk Firescaping. You have a lot of freedom when it comes to firescaping your property. Like I mentioned earlier, you can keep the greenery. You don't have to pave over everything and create an expensive, lifeless hardscape in order to be safe. Just design your lawn and garden with fuel breaks. Add retaining walls for safety and aesthetics, put pea gravel or pavers in the 0-5 zone, keep grasses cut short, keep trees from overhanging your driveway and leave 15 feet of clear roadway along your driveway and roadway for emergency vehicle access. If they can't fit their firetruck down your road or driveway, they won't try to force it. It's too much of a risk if flames may touch the side or top of the truck and they'll go to the next access point. Also consider any locked gates you may have. If they're electric, the wiring will likely fail from the heat and they can't access your property. If you have a gate that's manually locked, leave it unlocked and open so they can gain access. Same goes for your doors. Leave them unlocked, but securely shut, in case they need to hunker down inside.

The general rule of thumb for the intermediate zone is to simply have *discontinuous* tree and shrub canopies. So think of it like this: instead of having a dense jungle of greenery and it's a wild sea of greenery, give yourself a pathway to walk between everything and give large individuals, or groups, of plants room to thrive. Have little islands of manicured beauty or carefully tended chaos. Your property can be both beautiful and fire safe. When embers are raining down and your garden is at risk, it's better to keep the flames contained and lose one or two plots, rather than everything because they were all touching.

Specific recommendations are to keep tree canopies 10 feet apart in the intermediate zone. This is to help reduce the risk of scorching or igniting a tree if its neighbor is on fire. The goal is to keep crown fires far from the home or other structures, and get the flames back down on the ground where they burn with a lower intensity and burn out faster.

For shrubs and bushes the recommendation is 2x the width of the plant. It's kind of like social distancing: where we want one wingspan between us and a stranger, plants want twice their width between them and a neighbor.

Now if you're on a slope, those distances change. If you have a 20-40% incline, you want 4x the width between bushes and shrubs and 20 feet between individual or clumps of trees. On really extreme slopes, anything steeper than a 40% grade, you want 6x the width between shrubs and up to 30 feet between trees. When you factor in flame height and wind on these slopes, you need more distance to create a buffer for any potential flame or firebrand spread.

Another really important thing to consider: if you're located

INTERMEDIATE ZONE (5-30 FEET)

on a steep hill, it would behoove you to get some kind of retaining wall built up-slope of your home to catch any burning debris that rolls downhill. It would be awful if you followed all the steps and did everything right, and some burning material came rolling down and came to rest right up next to your home and ignited your siding. So take a look at your property. What's your topography? What's your ecology? Are you surrounded by rocks? Highly combustible plants? Are you at the bottom of a ravine? What extra steps might you need to take that someone in a different housing complex wouldn't have to worry about? It's all part of planning for the worst, and hoping for the best.

Before we move on to the extended zone, let's address some burning questions. No pun intended. A lot of people love mulch. But I just said it's a one hour fuel so it's bad right? That depends on your risk tolerance and what kind of mulch you're using. If you use mulch, or you have leaf litter and duff material on your property, that is ok. As long as it's not in that 0-5 foot range. In a lot of forest types, it's perfectly natural to have a layer of duff material on the ground. It was nature's original mulch. The thing is, now we have to balance that combustible material with sprawling housing developments, climate change, and years of fire suppression that allowed that duff layer to get too deep. Anything over 3 inches deep becomes a potential hazard. If and when that layer catches fire, it's more likely to smolder and have a sneaky low flame that may get missed by firefighters. This means two things: the heat can get trapped in the soil for longer which damages soil biota and soil health, and it becomes an insulated pocket of heat that can be extremely dangerous and re-ignite combustible material even days after the wildfire has passed.

So all the bacteria, fungi, worms, and other critters that live in the soil that are essential for a healthy, functioning soil system either get cooked or burrow really deep into the soil for safety. That leaves you with that ultra fine ash and dirt that gets everywhere. And that's when you see issues with compaction, erosion, landslides, and decreased water quality. So please keep that in mind if you feel like mitigation professionals are being unreasonable when they advise you against using combustible mulches. But, if you really want to use mulch, refer to the study from the University of Nevada Extension Office and the USDA.

The quick and dirty of it is they used 6 different types of mulch at a depth of 2-3" inches: composted wood chips, medium sized pine bark nuggets, pine needles, shredded rubber, shredded cedar, and mixed chips and plant biomass. The mixed chips had three variations: 3" of depth treated with fire retardant material, 3" of depth untreated, and 1" of depth untreated.

What they found was: the shredded rubber was the most hazardous mulch material: it had the highest flame height - averaging over 3 feet - and the highest temperature - reaching 630 degrees Fahrenheit. It ignited easily and burned intensely for a much longer time than the natural mulch materials.

The pine needles and shredded cedar were fairly comparable: both spread flame rapidly, at almost 50 feet per minute, and had temperatures just under 400 degrees Fahrenheit. Flame length for the pine needles were taller than the cedar, which reached almost a foot on average. The shredded cedar produced embers that ignited neighboring plots of mulch, where the pine needles did not.

The bark nuggets had one of the lowest rates of spread, but had one of the tallest flame heights and temperatures similar to that of the pine needles and shredded cedar.

The mixed chips at 3 inches of depth were nearly identical for temperature and flame height, but the treated chips had a significantly slower rate of flame spread. The mixed chips at 1 inch of depth had the second lowest temperature, flame height, and rate of spread behind the composted wood chips. The composted wood chips had almost no flame and instead smoldered slowly, estimated at a rate of about 4" per minute. Because the smoldering occurred unevenly through the 3 inch layers, it didn't always show signs of combustion on the top layer of mulch, but was spreading at lower levels.

All of these things considered, it would be advisable to keep mulch layers around an inch deep, as you'll still get 80-100% ground cover, and any ignition that occurs will be more visible when you return home, thus posing less of a burn risk or re-ignition risk if handled, moved, or mixed with other material that may have ignition potential left.

The moral of the mulch story is: you can have your mulch and landscaping, too. You just need to be aware of the risks associated with different kinds of mulch so you can make an informed decision around your personal risk tolerance levels.

4

The Extended Zone (30-100 feet)

Here, you can let things stay a little more wild. The rules get more relaxed, but it's still a good idea to keep things properly managed. The forests you see today are overgrown and have been mismanaged for the last 150 years. I know we all like our trees, but we've let them get over crowded, and just like with people, too many in too small a space leads to disease, pests, over-competition for available resources, and eventually leads to collapse. We need to start actively managing all of our property and restoring the natural balance of landscape and fire.

As well, with too many trees all competing for the same amount of water, consider how much more water could go back into our aquifers, wells, rivers and lakes if we had the natural balance of trees on our landscape. Grasslands, forests, and fire are all on a continuous cycle that can take anywhere from a few decades, to a couple hundred years, or in some very unique ecosystems up to one thousand years to complete and start over. The cycle of renewal doesn't happen on our (human) timescale, but we can help restore the balance and mitigate

THE EXTENDED ZONE (30-100 FEET)

total destruction in wildland urban areas. It's going to take time, money, and effort. But *more hands makes for lighter work.*

Ultimately, what you do with your extended zone is largely up to you. These are my recommendations:

1. Hire a local forester to assess your property. They'll be able to tell you what habitat and ecosystem type you live in, what flora and fauna you want to support and how. They should also have a solid understanding of the successional stages in your area and where your property needs to be on that spectrum to maximize fire resilience and greater landscape health. If your forester incorporates Indigenous Knowledge into their assessments and planning, that's an even bigger bonus. You can find them in the private and public sector through your local University Extension Office, Dept of Natural Resources or similar office, or even your local University Forestry or Plant Pathology Departments. Plenty of students eager for some real world experience would love to talk to you about your trees.

2. Make a design plan. Make sure your tree canopies are discontinuous (where appropriate) to help slow an approaching fire and decrease its intensity/severity. Some ecosystems have adapted to burn completely once every 100 years (1988 Yellowstone Lodgepole Forests). Others have adapted to burn low and slow every decade or so (Ponderosa Forests in the Rocky Mountains). Know your ecosystem and set your property mitigation/thinning goals.

3. Get to work. Whether you take a chainsaw or heavy equipment out, or you hire a crew, now's the time to turn words into action. Let the mechanical restoration begin and watch the beauty of a managed landscape unfold before your eyes.

Like I mentioned earlier, if you live on a small or narrow plot, and your home ignition zones overlap with those of your neighbors, don't fret. A lot of modern building materials have been manufactured to withstand high heat and direct flame exposure. Not indefinitely, but if you have overlapping zones or a neighbor who puts you at risk, you can still protect yourself and be reasonably confident in the survivability of your home. Just remember your Class A ratings and check out the open flame studies conducted by Dr. Jack Cohen and the Insurance Institute for Building and Home Safety (IBHS) and mitigate/retrofit accordingly. Check out our website for the latest building material research.

By now you should have a pretty good idea of what your home and property should look like to be considered ready for wildfire. You've got adequate spacing between plants, you've removed ladder fuels. Now you just have to make sure that all tree limbs are trimmed to at least 6 feet off the ground, and all dead material that may be hiding in bushes or shrubs gets cleared out and composted or burned. Some plants like juniper are very messy and will collect dead, dry material within its branches and near its base which makes it highly flammable and gives the fire extra fuel to burn extra hot. Their seed pods have been reported to explode and also burn extremely hot. The better you maintain your property and your plants, the more likely it is to survive a fire. I'll go over fire tolerant and highly flammable plants in a future book.

In that same vein, consider planting native species on your property. They're already adapted to that local climate and the local fire regime, and out west, a number of them are serotinous, meaning they need fire in some capacity in order to propagate.

THE EXTENDED ZONE (30-100 FEET)

For example, a number of pine tree species need fire to melt the resin on its cones so the seeds can be released. And it's great for local fish and wildlife to have native species for food, nests, and cover. Native plants have better symbiotic relationships with the local soil biota and are better at preventing erosion. Your local plants, animals, soil biota, and fungi have all evolved together for thousands of years. Let them help make your property more resilient to fire by not replacing them with unnatural fertilizers and non native plants.

If we work with nature to restore the balance, we'll all be much safer and much healthier.

A quick google search should yield some results for native plant nurseries and local experts from your University Extension office or environmental consultants.

As a final note, if you are interested in building and lighting your own burn piles, it is recommended that they be no bigger than six feet wide by six feet long by 6 feet high. And that is the absolute maximum. They must be far removed from all homes and structures and neighboring tree canopies so as not to scorch the lower branches of trees in the area or ignite any structures. If you don't have room for massive flames, start small. No shame in having small burn piles if it means keeping your fire under control and not being the reason the neighborhood burns down. Consider the amount of space you have to safely burn and keep your piles conservative. It's much preferable to toast marshmallows than get roasted by the court system.

And make sure you're in contact with your local fire department and any other federal agency like the forest service or bureau of land management to **get a burn permit** and make sure you're burning at the appropriate time. Local foresters or fire departments can also alert you to any changes in condition that would render it unsafe to burn such as changes in wind speed or direction or relative humidity.

5

Insurance

One of the most difficult things I've heard from homeowners who've experienced loss, is the struggle they had with insurance.

If you get nothing else out of this book, I hope you remember that *insurance is not your friend.* It doesn't matter if you and your insurance agent are buddies and get lunch - when there's nothing left but ashes, they don't have the power or the authority to write you a blank check to recover what you lost. And with the growing number of claims, insurance companies have had to deal with over the last few years, they're going to do everything they can to cancel or decrease coverage. Especially in locales where landlords are price gouging the markets and charging exorbitant amounts in monthly rent because "insurance will pay for it." Games like that will cost us all. Profiting off of other people's losses is vile and reprehensible, and the long term consequences will be felt by everyone.

Step 1. Call your insurance company and review your coverage! With the way the housing market has been, you need to know if the policy you got 20 years ago on a house you bought for $150,00 will cover your rebuilding expenses now that your home is worth $750,000.

Step 1.5. Take stock of everything you own. Head over the Adaptive Firescapes webpage and download the documents we've created for you. Fill out the checklist for everything you own. Be sure to include any upgrades, remodels, and DIY projects that have increased your home's value and need to be covered. Don't forget any special policy riders for jewelry, fine art, collectibles, weapons, etc.

Step 2. Determine what new policies/riders you might need:

2.1. **Dwelling Coverage**: this makes sure you have coverage to repair or replace your home, garage, deck, shed or other structure. ***Make sure you establish that this specifically covers wildfire!*** A lot of policies will only cover fires that start *inside* the home. Homeowners find out when it's too late that they didn't have *wildfire* coverage. Make sure this covers other structures, too. Some Dwelling Coverage policies will cover a shed or detached garage, and some won't.

2.2. **Additional Living Expenses Coverage:** this will help pay for rent if you become displaced due to partial damage and remodel or due to complete loss. Verify how much you'll receive monthly, and how many months you'll receive the support.

Some things to keep in mind: I've heard horror stories about construction workers walking off job sites (people's new homes) to go work for another company that's paying a higher wage. In this new era where everything is in flux, a lot of people are motivated by their financial needs, especially post COVID. They have to look out for their best interests, and that may not always coincide with your need for your house to be rebuilt on a certain timeline. Be aware of worker strikes too: truckers, loggers/sawyers, lumber mills, etc. Consider all the mills that have shut down over the last 2 decades due to political pressure and policy changes and how that can bottleneck lumber supply and keep prices high. There are so many factors at play. With about 1 out of 3 Americans being at high risk from wildfire, we can't afford to have millions of people all be in need at the same time. And that's not including people affected by hail, tornadoes, flooding, or hurricanes. Keep the big picture in mind when you're trying to figure out a rebuilding timeline. There are people who become permanently homeless/displaced after a wildfire. I don't want to see you be one of them.

2.3. **Personal Property Coverage**: this will help pay for personal items you may need replaced like clothes, kitchen goods, and furniture.

2.4.**Landscaping Coverage**: if you've spent a lot of money creating a beautiful landscape around your home, you may want to consider covering the cost of replacing it.

Step 3. Make sure you have **flood insurance**. Sounds crazy. You just had a massive fire. What on earth are we thinking about floods for? It's not uncommon, especially after a severe fire, for flash floods and massive debris flows to cause more chaos. When all the vegetation has burned away and soil and ash are exposed to the elements, rain will wash right off the landscape and take everything with it.

You can see backcountry examples of this on our website. When I was working in remote parts of Idaho, we came across major damage in our forests: unbelievable erosion and staggering log jams piled up on eroded mountainsides.

When severe fires are followed by rainfall and we have disaster after disaster, recovery becomes much more difficult. That applies to urban communities too. Consider hillsides washing away, roads or bridges washing out, power and other utilities being interrupted, massive land and water contamination from chemicals in our homes and businesses.

For more information on what to do for your business insurance should it pertain to you, go to our website and download the checklist.

About the Author

Nicole Henningfeld is a wildfire mitigation professional versed in home hardening, defensible space/hazardous fuels reduction, building codes, and fire ecology. As such, she is developing educational materials for homeowners and professionals in various industries from construction to city planning. Having spent most of her life in California and Montana, she's watched how fire affects the social and physical landscapes and wants to help shape the way we adapt to an ever changing world.

You can connect with me on:
- https://adaptivefirescapes.com
- https://www.facebook.com/profile.php?id=100091885516142